MW01142122

GOD IS
A FOUR-LETTER
WORD

GOD IS
A FOUR-LETTER
WORD

John W. Whitehead

TRI PRESS®
Charlottesville, VA

God Is A Four-Letter Word

Printed in the United States of America by TRI PRESS®

For information, contact:
TRI PRESS
Post Office Box 7482
Charlottesville, VA 22906-7482

ISBN: 978-0-9772331-4-4

Scripture quotations are taken from the
New International Version.

Book design by Chris Combs

Whoever does not love does not know God, because God is love.

—I John 4:8

If I speak in the tongues of men and of angels, but have not love, I am only a resounding gong or a clanging cymbal. If I have the gift of prophecy and can fathom all mysteries and all knowledge, and if I have a faith that can move mountains, but have not love, I am nothing. If I give all I possess to the poor and surrender my body to the flames, but have not love, I gain nothing. Love is patient, love is kind. It does not envy, it does not boast, it is not proud. It is not rude, it is not self-seeking, it is not easily angered, it keeps no record of wrongs. Love does not delight in evil but rejoices with the truth. It always protects, always trusts, always hopes, always perseveres. Love never fails. But where there are prophecies, they will cease; where there are tongues, they will be stilled; where there is knowledge, it will pass away. For we know in part and we prophesy in part, but when perfection comes, the imperfect disappears. When I was a child, I talked like a child, I thought like a child, I reasoned like a child. When I became a man, I put childish ways behind me. Now we see but a poor reflection as in a mirror; then we shall see face to face. Now I know in part; then I shall know fully, even as I am fully known. And now these three remain: faith, hope and love. But the greatest of these is love.

—I Corinthians 13:1-13

CONTENTS

ACKNOWLEDGMENTS

Among the many fine people who have helped me over the years, two stand out. The first is my wife, Carol, whose nimble fingers type my work. Carol's advice on what I put on paper is always helpful.

Second, there is Nisha Mohammed. Nisha, who has worked with me some fifteen years now, is a good friend and a valuable editor. Without her help, much of what I write would not rise to the level it does.

Thus, thank you Carol and Nisha. And thanks to all those who have, over the years, supported me in my endeavors.

CHAPTER ONE
If Anyone Loves Me

One of the problems with humanists is that they tend to "love" humanity as a whole—Man with a capital M, Man as an idea—but forget about man as an individual, as a person. Christianity is to be exactly the opposite. Christianity is not to love in abstraction, but to love the individual who stands before me in a person-to-person relationship. He must never be faceless to me or I am denying everything I say I believe. This concept will always involve some cost. It is not a cheap thing, because we live in a fallen world, and we ourselves are fallen.

> —Francis Schaeffer,
>   *True Spirituality* (1971)

If anyone loves me, he will obey my teaching. My Father will love him, and we will come to him and make our home with him. He who does not love me will not obey my teaching. These words you hear are not my own; they belong to the Father who sent me.

> —John 14:23-24

I became a Christian at the age of 28. And, like everything in my life, I jumped into Christianity with both feet. Having been what some would call a bleeding heart liberal prior to my conversion, it logically followed that I would use my legal knowledge and training as a constitutional attorney to become an advocate for oppressed and persecuted Christians.

During those early days after starting The Rutherford Institute in 1982, I came to know a number of leaders in the Christian socio-political movement. I worked alongside the influential Christian theologian Francis Schaeffer. I stayed in the home of Christian Reconstructionist and father of the Christian Right R.J. Rushdoony. I rubbed shoulders with Jerry Falwell, Pat Robertson, James Dobson and Tim LaHaye, co-founder of the Moral Majority and co-author of the bestselling *Left Behind* novels, among others. Thus, I was present when Christianity in America was metastasizing into the political behemoth it is today.

For years, I completely bought into what the Christian Right had to say about Christianity. Then I slowly began to realize that the brand of Christianity being practiced by many within the so-called "Moral Majority" had little to do with what Christ taught.

In the years since becoming a Christian, I have struggled to reconcile the teachings of the itinerant preacher with the Christianity practiced by those who claim to speak for God, and this book is a reflection of that struggle. More importantly, it is a roadmap of my journey back to the Jesus of the New Testament.

This book, in many ways, is a personal statement; some thoughts on what I have learned about what it means to be a Christian. And this is what I believe: Jesus Christ was good. He was caring. He had powerful, profound things to say—things that would change how we view people, alter government policies and change the world. He went around helping the poor. And when confronted by those in authority, he did not shy away from speaking truth to power. He never identified with the powerful. Instead, he identified with the outcasts of society. He taught that God is love and emphasized forgiveness, compassion and reaching out to the poor.

I am not an expert on Christianity. I am not even a trained theologian, but neither was Jesus. Nor can I promise that I am any better than the next person in terms of perfectly practicing my faith. Indeed, I am living proof of all of life's contradictions. But I am a Christian—an imperfect one, certainly, as are all who call themselves by that name. And as I have read, studied and prayed, I have been reminded that Christ still speaks truth to power. He still extends love and compassion to a hurting world. And just as there are those who pervert the teachings of Jesus, there are also those who are witnesses to what he taught—people who live out their faith, rather than talking it to death. And although there are many who will disagree with what I have to say, I believe it must be said. After all, the truth is what we are after. And that truth is found in the teachings of Christ. As Jesus said, "If you hold to my teaching, you are really my disciples. Then you will know the truth, and the truth will set you free" (John 8:31-32).

Jesus was a radical and a revolutionary. He showed the world that it was possible to undermine an empire of force with love and compassion. He gave hope to the downtrodden, the outcast and the poor—the hope that truth, in the end, would win out. This hope has inspired many through the centuries to persevere against all odds.

In the 2000-plus years since Christ walked the earth, much has changed: man has built skyscrapers, crossed great distances, conquered the sea and sky. And yet even with our greatest inventions and most advanced technologies, nothing compares to the teachings of the carpenter from Galilee—the greatest of which is this: love conquers all.

Love litters the musical landscape, is the basis of all lasting human relationships and is the very essence, we are told, of God Himself. It is the one thing we all long for both in our human relationships and in our relationship with the Divine. Why, then, do we so often fail at love? Why does it seem always beyond our reach? Could it be that we fail at love because we don't understand what it means to *truly* love one another?

Unfortunately, love as it is practiced by many today pales in comparison to the love shown by Christ. Greeting card commercials, Hollywood movies and our own meager understanding of love cause us to fall back on trite platitudes, empty gestures and nice words, all the while missing the heart of the message. But as the Gospel of John tells us, love is in the doing, in the way Christians follow Jesus. It is how we obey him. But actually loving our fellow human beings, not to mention God, can be one of the most difficult tasks imaginable. Sometimes, in fact, it is nigh to impossible. Even so, Jesus commands us to love at all costs.

Jesus' life was a lesson in how to love our fellow human beings. Too often, however, we focus solely on those episodes in which Jesus acted compassionately or mercifully. Yet while these are important facets of love, they are only part of the picture. Love as Jesus lived it is neither pretty nor easy. There were other aspects of love modeled by Jesus during his life—aspects that we too often overlook—such as a willingness to speak truth to power, selflessness, righteous anger, a rejection of material wealth and a disregard for power, politics and celebrity. Jesus' brand of love is courageous, bold, sacrificial, compassionate, humble, charitable, just and nonviolent.

Thus, I would venture to say that in gaining a better understanding of the nature of love—as practiced by Jesus—and in heeding the simple truths of the itinerant preacher from Galilee, we might find the faith that can transform the world. Only then can we hope to "turn the world upside down." Such is our quest in the following pages.

CHAPTER TWO
Jesus Speaks Still

Every happening, great and small, that is to
say, is a parable whereby God speaks to us: and
the art of life is to get the message.
   —Malcolm Muggeridge,
   Christ and the Media (1977)

Blessed are those who hunger and thirst for
righteousness, for they will be filled.
   —Matthew 5:6

The story of the birth, life and death of Jesus Christ, which has been called "the greatest story ever told," has resonated, both consciously and subconsciously, throughout Western history. It has been retold time and again in every medium, from poetry and prose to art, music and film, by Christians and non-Christians alike.

Take, for example, the 2006 film *Children of Men*, a cautionary tale set in 2027 in and around a dystopian London fractious with violence and warring nationalistic sects. Animal corpses litter the countryside, and people with agendas are always blowing up something. Non-native residents are rounded up by the British government and shipped off to refugee camps or worse, all for the good of the state. In the midst of this, humankind, which can no longer procreate, faces the likelihood of extinction, as the world's youngest citizen has just died at the age of 18. With the discovery of a miraculously pregnant woman, an activist agrees to protect her from government agents who may want to murder both her and her child. He helps transport her to a sanctuary at sea, where the child's birth may enable scientists to save the future of humankind and restore faith for a future beyond for those presently on earth.

The parallels to the Christ story, in which the miraculous birth of a child heralds hope for the future of humankind, are evident. As the New Testament tells it, a child was born to a poor Jewish woman at a time when the Hebrew people were longing and praying for someone to free them from Roman oppression. The miracle of the child's birth is announced by an angel, who proclaims that the child will be called Jesus. After journeying to the city of Bethlehem, the woman gives birth to the child in a stable. Then she, the baby Jesus and Joseph, the man appointed to protect them, become refugees and are forced to flee the country to escape the wrath of King Herod, who has ordered the child found and killed. Thus, even as a baby, the very presence of Jesus was subversive.

From the beginning, there was something special about this Jesus. He was a message from God to a world torn apart by violence, oppression, persecution and civil unrest. And the message was one of love, forgiveness, compassion and what came to be called the Christmas hope: "Peace on earth, Good will toward men."

People the world over continue to look to Jesus with faith and hope for the future. Yet not much is known about him beyond what is recounted in the Bible. We are told that he grew to be a man and became a lay carpenter. And the specialness of the child eventually manifested itself in the man, who became a prophet and offered some of the most profound teachings ever heard. However, Jesus' teachings, which tended to undermine the basic foundation of the governmental, religious and societal institutions of the day, were seen as a threat to those in power—the Romans and even the Jewish religious leaders of Israel. In fact, his teachings and how he acted were considered so revolutionary that the authorities conspired to do away with the irritating carpenter.

As the narrative goes, Jesus was sentenced to death and crucified on a cross. Only the worst criminals were put to death in such a cruel and inhumane way. Yet even in death, Jesus showed his specialness. Indeed, although he was rejected by his own people (when given the choice, they called for a man accused of murder to be pardoned rather than Jesus) and eventually slain by the Roman Empire, Jesus was resurrected to live in the hearts of people forever. Thus, what looked like a disastrous end—humiliating death on a cross—became a source of triumph and hope for future generations.

Incredibly, despite the violent end to his life, the message of Jesus' life, death and probably his most enigmatic teaching—a breakpoint in history—is that "God is love." Jesus' proclamations on love and community have since become a source of freedom for the underclasses—the outcasts and forsaken. As Cambridge University professor Michael Grant notes in his book *Jesus* (2004), "The most potent figure, not only in the history of religion, but in world history as a whole, is Jesus Christ: the maker of one of the few revolutions which have lasted. Millions of men and women for century after century have found his life and teachings overwhelmingly significant and moving."

Indeed, for centuries, people in the West have looked to the Christian story to discover the meaning of life—that is, where they came from, how much they were valued, why they were here, how they should live and what lay beyond death. This story of a poor man who stressed a compassionate view of humanity has given hope to the downtrodden, the outcast and the poor. It has stirred great men to be deliverers and even sacrifice their lives for what they believed. This was epitomized by early Christians who overcame what seemed to be insurmountable obstacles and who practiced an observable and practical love that, without reservation, cut across all lines—language, nationality, age, color of skin, education, economic levels, class and so on. Indeed, the early Christian church, before it was institutionalized, cut across the barriers that divided men—Jew and Greek, Greek and barbarian, male and female; from master to slave; from the naturally proud Gentiles of Macedonia to the proud Jews who called Gentiles dogs.

Without this story of liberation, much of the Western world, including the United States, would still be under the curse of slavery. For instance, the Christian story was the basis of Martin Luther King's fight for the equality of black Americans—a struggle that changed the face of the country. As Reverend King proclaimed, "There are some who still find the cross a stumbling block, and others consider it foolishness, but I am more convinced than ever before that it is the power of God unto social and individual salvation."

Such was the spiritual dynamic of the Christian story as proclaimed by people such as King. Yet, from the beginning, King found himself in opposition to church leaders who should have been proclaiming the self-same message of love, hope and freedom. In April 1963, while serving a jail sentence for participating in civil rights demonstrations, King wrote his famous "Letter from Birmingham City Jail" in response to eight prominent white Alabama clergymen who had called on African-Americans to cease their civil disobedience and let the courts handle the problem of segregation. King's words reminded Americans that the early church—the church established by Jesus' followers—would never have been content to remain silent while injustice and persecution ruled the land:

There was a time when the church was very powerful. It was during that period when the early Christians rejoiced when they were deemed worthy to suffer for what they believed. In those days the church was not merely a thermometer that recorded the ideas and principles of popular opinion; it was a thermostat that transformed the mores of society. Wherever the early Christians entered a town the power structure got disturbed and immediately sought to convict them for being "disturbers of the peace" and "outside agitators".... They brought an end to such ancient evils as infanticide and gladiatorial contest.

Today's church, King points out, stands in stark contrast to the early church. Today, the church "is so often the arch-supporter of the status quo. Far from being disturbed by the presence of the church, the power structure of the average community is consoled by the church's silent and often vocal sanction of things as they are."

What's more, too often the church today falls into the trap of compartmentalizing Jesus and reducing his teachings to simple platitudes. The people sing the refrain that "God is love" and "we are to love our neighbor," but they frequently fail to act on it. But as Jesus recognized in his own time: "Not everyone who says to me, 'Lord, Lord,' will enter the kingdom of heaven, but only he who does the will of my Father who is in heaven" (Matthew 7:21).

Meaningful Spirituality

Some of the finest people I know are not those who profess to be Christians. Despite never having made a confession of faith in Jesus Christ, these non-Christians come closest to reflecting the teachings of Jesus in what they say and how they live their lives. Indeed, they reflect the type of compassion that should be practiced by all who call themselves Christians.

Unfortunately, the reverse is also true. Some who call themselves followers of Jesus Christ least embody the spirits of compassion, charity, love and humility that are the hallmarks of a true Christian. In fact, they often give Christianity a bad name. Since becoming a Christian in 1974, I have had a front-row seat for the best and worst that Christianity has to offer. And many times, the things I've witnessed being done "in the name of Jesus Christ" have sorely tested my faith.

But I am not alone in this struggle. Prophetically, some might say, Martin Luther King predicted that "if the church of today does not recapture the sacrificial spirit of the early church, it will…be dismissed as an irrelevant social club with no meaning." With rampant materialism that engulfs so much of the church, coupled with scandals and waning attendance, many of today's churches have, in effect, given truth to King's vision.

Transcendence, meaning and spirituality are seldom found in many churches today. In their place is a religion that attempts to tame the radical Jesus and cut him down to size—where logic is often the enemy and truth is a menace. And increasingly, more and more people are expressing their discontent with the state of Christianity today. Indeed, there is a growing sense that a vital part of Christianity has been lost. In its place is a brand of religion that bears little resemblance to the teachings of Jesus.

"Christianity today often resembles an egg into which someone has poked a hole and sucked out all its contents," writes author Richard Smoley in *Forbidden Faith: The Gnostic Legacy from the Gospels to the DaVinci Code* (2006), "and then taken the shell, encrusted it with gold and jewels, and set it up as an object of veneration. In many ways, it remains a beautiful shell, but more and more people are finding that it no longer offers any nourishment. If they complain, they're usually told that they just need to have more faith—which is of course no answer at all."

Indeed, there is a growing sense that somewhere between the time that Jesus walked the earth and the church of the present day, a vital part of Christianity has been lost. In its place is a brand of religion that often bears little resemblance to the teachings of Jesus.

This may be due, in part, because, according to a study conducted by the Barna Group, the "Christian body in America is immersed in a crisis of biblical illiteracy." For instance, Gary Burge, professor of New Testament at Wheaton College, writing for *Christianity Today*, notes that there is an increasingly lower standard of biblical literacy among his students, who represent almost every Protestant denomination in the U.S. In the research of incoming Wheaton undergraduates, several surprising statistics stand out—one-third of his students could not identify Matthew as an apostle from a list of New Testament names, and one-half did not know that the Christmas story is in the Book of Matthew.

And journalist Bill McKibben in a 2005 article in *Harper's* magazine writes: "Only 40 percent of Americans can name four of the Ten Commandments, and a scant half can cite any of the four authors of the Gospels. Twelve percent believe Joan of Arc was Noah's wife." Furthermore:

> Three quarters of Americans believe the Bible teaches that "God helps those who help themselves." That is, three out of four

Americans believe that this uber-American idea, a notion at the core of our current individualist politics and culture, which was in fact uttered by Ben Franklin, actually appears in Holy Scripture. The thing is, not only is Franklin's wisdom not biblical; it's counter-biblical. Few ideas could be further from the gospel message, with its radical summons to love of neighbor. On this essential matter, most Americans—most American Christians—are simply wrong, as if 75 percent of American scientists believed that Newton proved gravity causes apples to fly up.

Thus, although Americans—including Christians—claim to revere the Bible, by and large they don't read it. Moreover, as King and others have recognized, the Christian story no longer grips Western imagination as it once did.

Time magazine reflected the mood of King's day quite aptly on April 10, 1966, with its sepulchral red-on-black cover that asked, "Is God Dead?" *Time*'s cover appeared as the death-of-God movement was peaking. Its opening paragraph set the tone: "Is God dead? It is a question that tantalizes both believers, who perhaps secretly fear that he is, and the atheists, who possibly suspect that the answer is no." The article's ending sentence is an epitaph for the modern age: "Perhaps today, the Christian can do no better than echo the prayer of the worried father who pleaded with Christ to heal his spirit-possessed son: 'I believe, help my unbelief.'"

However, it wasn't that God was dead in 1966. Rather, the Christian story, at least as it was being lived out at the time, was becoming less relevant and compelling. In fact, as early as the 1960s, it became apparent not only to men such as Martin Luther King but also to the youth movement that what passed for Christianity provided few, if any, solutions to the problems confronting them—most of which were spiritual.

Thus, people began deserting the church. Great Britain is reflective of the trend that emerged. In 1940, 36 percent of British children attended Sunday school. In 1960, it was 24 percent. By 2000, it was 4 percent. A recent study tracks a similar trend in the United States. In fact, in the past 40 years, denominations have increasingly reported a decline in their numbers. The most realistic data indicates that less than 18 percent of Americans now regularly attend church.

Add to this the fact that young people have been increasingly turning away from the church. According to a 2003 study conducted by the Barna Research Group, "millions of twentysomething

Americans—many of whom were active in churches during their teens—pass through their most formative adult decade while putting Christianity on the backburner." Indeed, the study points out that "the most striking reality of twentysomethings' faith is their relative absence from Christian churches," showing that only 3 out of 10 people in their twenties attend church in a typical week. According to David Kinnamen, a Barna researcher, "Although it may come across as unwarranted skepticism, young adults are questioning their church experience in some legitimate ways."

The brand of Christianity that is touted on television, from the pulpits of mega-churches and over the airwaves has little relevance to their lives. Nor does it offer much in the way of hope, truth or beauty. Yet, even so, the human instinct for fellowship, ritual, worship and spirituality has not disappeared. After all, religion, when stripped of its dogmatism and materialism, reflects a hunger for meaning and spiritual transcendence, a desire to regain our innocence and sense of wonder. That was what Jesus may have meant when he said that "unless you change and become like little children, you will never enter the kingdom of heaven" (Matthew 18:3).

Religion serves a vital purpose in a society—to cement the structure of society, upholding the values and ideals that preserve the common good, thereby binding individuals both to God and to one another. Thus, when religion fails its basic purposes, as we have seen with modern Christianity, a spiritual void is created and those who hunger for spirituality and transcendence are forced to seek new forms.

The fact is that people are desperate for genuine spirituality and transcendence. Many still want to know God or a God-force. Seeking spirituality, they investigate the occult, astrology charts, angels, UFOs and extraterrestrial beings—anything to fill the void. This hunger is also reflected in the number of individuals seeking comfort in alternative religions, in addictions, in alternative lifestyles—the list goes on and on.

Eastern teachings that stress the need for spiritual experience—that is, the need for genuinely religious people to verify within themselves what they have heard or read—have spread in mass culture to such a degree that words like Zen, karma, yin and yang and feng shui are now part of our standard vocabulary. While Eastern religions are still prominent in the new millennium, they are now vying with New Age religions, Wicca and Islam. In fact, reports claim that Islam is "one of the fastest growing religions" in the United States. And by 2010, the number of Muslims in America is expected to surpass the Jewish population, making Islam the country's second-largest faith after Christianity.

Hedonistic consumerism and self-preservation are now celebrated. This is reflected in the obsessive interest in the body through exercise, diet and vitamins and in personal identity, self-fulfillment and authenticity issues—all now also advocated on so-called "Christian" television. Popular entertainment, television (and now the Internet), politics, sports, celebrities, drugs, sex and so on are also being used to fill the spiritual void.

Clearly, today's church is failing to meet the spiritual hunger of the society around it. Consequently, we are seeing a backlash against all things associated with traditional religion, particularly evangelical Christianity. For example, those of the Christian Right, with whom a large percentage of evangelicals identify, are being called "fascists" and the "American Taliban." Indeed, as I write these words, Christopher Hitchens' book *god is not Great: How Religion Poisons Everything* (2007) is one of the best-selling books in America.

Recent high-profile scandals involving Christians whose integrity and morality have been called into question also underscore the crisis in modern Christianity. Such scandals, however, are merely the by-product of a graver problem. Modern Christianity, having lost sight of Jesus' teachings, has accommodated itself to the spirit of the age. And it has been co-opted by an acerbic dogmatism, materialism and politics. Simply put, it has lost its spirituality.

CHAPTER THREE
Speaking Truth to Power

The Powers are inextricably locked into God's system, whose human face is revealed by Jesus. They are answerable to God. And that means that every subsystem in the world is, in principle, redeemable. Nothing is outside the redemptive care and transforming love of God.

—Walter Wink, *The Powers That Be:*
Theology for a New Millennium (1998)

You are right in saying I am a king. In fact, for this reason I was born, and for this I came into the world, to testify to the truth. Everyone on the side of truth listens to me.

—Jesus to Pilate, John 18:37

Disagreement, doubt and anxiety are pervasive around the world. Few societies or individuals enjoy untroubled certitude. And judging from the disorder in the world, few societies or individuals have any real concept of truth upon which to live their lives. "At the same time, the Christian understanding of things has to an astonishing degree been forgotten," writes professor Glenn Tinder in *The Political Meaning of Christianity* (1989). "Even among professed Christians, not many are very sharply aware of the most distinctive insights into human nature and political life."

It is understandable, then, that many wonder whether Jesus Christ, and what he taught, has any relevance to the world in which we live and its weapons of mass destruction, threats of terrorism and growing militarization. After all, times are difficult. We live in an age of profound fear and confusion. As the pervasiveness of the state increases in Western countries in our post-9/11 world, freedom is increasingly being squelched. The reason, we are told, is to protect us and keep us safe.

Increasingly, surveillance cameras monitor virtually every area of our lives outside the privacy of our homes. The government now listens in on our telephone calls and reads our e-mails. Neighbors call the FBI to report those living next door for having a suspicious bumper sticker, and, incredibly, FBI agents investigate such matters. The President can now label anyone, including American citizens, "enemy combatants" and hold them indefinitely without access to family or an attorney. The Constitution and Bill of Rights are under attack. And as the threat of terrorism increases, the mantra for safety and security is drowning out any notion of true freedom.

Albert Einstein, in discussing hatred against the Jews, retold an ancient fable in his book *Ideas and Opinions* (1954):

> The shepherd boy said to the horse: "You are the noblest beast that treads the earth. You deserve to live in untroubled bliss; and indeed your happiness would be complete were it not for the treacherous stag. But he practiced from youth to excel you in fleetness of foot. His faster pace allows him to reach the water holes before you do. He and his tribe drink up the water far and wide, while you and your foal are left to thirst. Stay with me! My wisdom and guidance shall deliver you and your kind from a dismal and ignominious state."

> Blinded by envy and hatred of the stag, the horse agreed. He yielded to the shepherd lad's bridle. He lost his freedom and became

the shepherd's slave.

In America today, the state is the shepherd boy promising that if the people will only accept the bridle, the government will provide safety and deliver them from the terrorists. All it will cost is their loss of freedom. Similarly, as with the horse, Americans suffering the tribulations of hatred, bigotry, powerlessness, poverty and ignorance are also gullible prey for the easy fix of the government's promises.

Often, government promises come to us under the guise that "they are only working for our good." C. S. Lewis describes the problem in *God in the Dock* (1971):

> Of all tyrannies a tyranny sincerely exercised for the good of its victims may be the most oppressive. It may be better to live under robber barons than under omnipotent moral busybodies. The robber baron's cruelty may sometimes sleep, his cupidity may at some point be satiated; but those who torment us for our own good will torment us without end for they do so with the approval of their own conscience.

The point is that in the process of seeking perhaps even worthy goals, the foundational principles of freedom are being destroyed. Playwright Robert Bolt poses the dilemma in *A Man for All Seasons* (1960):

SIR THOMAS MOORE: Yes. What would you do? Cut a great road through the law to get after the Devil?

ROPER: I'd cut down every law in England to do that!

SIR THOMAS MOORE:.... Oh?.... And when the last law was down, and the Devil turned round on you—where would you hide, Roper, the laws all being flat?.... This country's planted thick with laws from coast to coast—man's laws, not God's—and if you cut them down...d'you really think you could stand upright in the winds that would blow then?

Sir Thomas Moore's logic applies as well when the "Devil" is racism, bigotry or terrorism. The government is cutting great roads through the very foundations of freedom to get after its modern devils, and this is the heart of the problem.

Yet we are not helpless in the face of this threat. This is where Jesus comes in. The greatest gift Jesus brought us both when he came into the world and by way of the cross was to give us true freedom. As I have grappled with the reality of life in an increasingly totalitarian state, I have come to realize that Jesus, his life and his teachings provide us with important lessons in what it means for Christians to be stewards of freedom and speak truth to power.

Speaking truth to power has inevitably, in the past, meant oppression and sometimes persecution. For Christ, it meant death. And yet, even knowing the price that would have to be paid, Jesus was never afraid to speak truth to power. In fact, Jesus denounced the most respected men of his day, such as the elders and chief priests of the Temple. And he was not afraid to go to the heart of the matter. Jesus, so to speak, was in their faces. As he told the Temple leaders, "I tell you the truth, the tax collectors and the prostitutes are entering the kingdom of God ahead of you" (Matthew 21:31).

The Government of God

On a spring day in the year 30, two processions entered Jerusalem. It was the beginning of the week of Passover, the most sacred week of the Jewish year. In centuries past, Christians have celebrated this day as Palm Sunday. For many, this week, which ends with Easter, is the most sacred week of the Christian year.

One was a peasant procession, the other an imperial Roman procession. From the East, Jesus rode a donkey down the Mount of Olives as his followers cheered. Jesus was from the peasant village of Nazareth, and his followers came from a peasant class that was considered beneath both the Jewish and Roman rulers.

On the opposite side of the city, from the West, Pontius Pilate, the Roman governor, entered Jerusalem at the head of a column of imperial soldiers and cavalrymen with pomp and circumstance. It was a statement of raw military might. As Marcus J. Borg and John Dominic Crossan write in *The Last Week: What the Gospels Really Teach About Jesus' Final Days in Jerusalem* (2006):

> Imagine the imperial procession's arrival in the city. A visual panoply of imperial power: cavalry on horses, foot soldiers, leather armor, helmets, weapons, banners, golden eagles mounted on poles, sun glinting on metal and gold. Sounds: the marching of feet, the creaking of leather, the clinking of bridles, the beating of drums. The swirling of dust. The eyes of the silent onlookers, some curious, some awed, some resentful.

Pilate's procession displayed not only imperial

power but also Roman imperial theology. The emperor was not simply the ruler of Rome; he was seen as the Son of God. Thus, for Rome's Jewish subjects, Pilate's procession embodied not only a rival social order but also a rival theology and, thus, a rival kingdom.

Jesus' procession, however, proclaimed a different kind of kingdom, a kingdom for here and now. As Christ teaches his disciples to pray, "your kingdom come, your will be done on earth as it is in heaven" (Matthew 6:10). This kingdom is based on love of humanity and peace where rulers were to be servants of the people. This was the kingdom of God.

Pilate's procession, however, proclaimed the power of empire—an empire of subjugation and violence where the people either obeyed or suffered. The two processions embodied the central conflict that led to Jesus' execution, and it is the same conflict that confronts Christians who dare speak the truth of Christ to power today.

As Jesus rode the donkey down the Mount of Olives to the city, he was surrounded by a throng of enthusiastic followers. They spread cloaks, strew leafy branches on the road and shouted, "Hosanna to the Son of David! Blessed is he who comes in the name of the Lord! Hosanna in the highest!" (Matthew 21:9). "Hosanna" is the Hebrew word meaning "Save, we pray."

The meaning of this demonstration has both political and religious connotations. It uses symbolism from the prophet Zechariah. According to Zechariah, a king would be coming to Jerusalem (Zion) "righteous and having salvation, gentle and riding on a donkey, on a colt, the foal of a donkey" (Zechariah 9:9). Zechariah 9:10 details what kind of king he will be:

> I will take away the chariots from Ephraim and the war-horses from Jerusalem, and the battle bow will be broken. He will proclaim peace to the nations. His rule will extend from sea to sea and from the River to the ends of the earth.

Jesus the king, riding on a donkey, will banish war and violence from the land—no more chariots, war-horses or bows. He was a king of peace.

The message to the powers-that-be, as Borg and Crossan note, was clear: "Jesus' procession deliberately countered what was happening on the other side of the city. Pilate's procession embodied the power, glory, and violence of the empire that ruled the world. Jesus' procession embodied an alternative vision, the kingdom of God."

This contrast—between the kingdom of God, based on love of people and peace, and the kingdom of Caesar, based on subjugating people and violence—is central to the story of Christ. As such, Jesus' procession that day symbolized his direct and subtle undermining of both the political and religious establishments that ruled the world.

Of course, the Romans eventually came to see Jesus as enough of a threat to have him killed. In the time of Jesus, religious preachers and self-proclaimed prophets were not summarily arrested and executed. Nor were nonviolent protesters. Indeed, the high priests and Roman governors in Jerusalem would normally allow a protest, particularly a small-scale one, to run its course. However, the authorities were quick to dispose of leaders and movements that even appeared to threaten the Roman Empire.

The charges leveled against Jesus—that he was a threat to the stability of the nation, opposed paying Roman taxes and claimed to be the rightful King as Messiah of Israel—were purely political, not religious. To the Romans, any one of these charges was enough to merit death by crucifixion. But the gravest charge, for which Jesus was ultimately crucified, was stated in the inscription on the cross: "The King of the Jews." The Roman governor Pontius Pilate, who alone had the authority to execute Jesus, focused on his political identity: "Are you the king of the Jews?" (Matthew 27:11). This seems to be primarily what mattered to Pilate, whose job it was to uphold the religious, as well as the temporal, power of the deified Caesars.

Jesus does not deny the allegation which, if true, will lead to his death. He answers: "You are right in saying I am a king. In fact, for this reason I was born, and for this I came into the world, to testify to the truth. Everyone on the side of truth listens to me" (John 18:37).

Jesus' proclamation of the kingdom of God—also known as the "government" of God—was a total reordering of both the spiritual and temporal life. Jesus' teaching on the government of God, as seen, for example, in the Sermon on the Mount, is that the significance of the rule of God pertains to everything—marriage, money, personal relationships, community life, religion, politics and so on. Jesus also addresses prayer, faith, repentance, forgiveness, honesty and our relationship to God. And although the government of God is far broader than politics, it has political ramifications. "The rule of God over everything is also God's rule over politics," writes Alan Storkey in *Jesus and Politics: Confronting the Powers* (2005). "It is the central truth of political life, the reference point for states, rulers, law, and justice—whether they recognize it or not. Logic requires it. How could the rule of God not apply to states and politics, as though God opted out of this part of their existence?"

Incredibly, Jesus had entered Jerusalem riding a donkey, proclaiming the government of God and eventually laying it all before the people and their rulers. That is why Jesus was able to say to Pilate: "You would have no power over me if it were not given to you from above" (John 19:11). Earlier, Jesus had told his followers not to fear rulers because they can only kill you (Matthew 10:28). Now standing before the Roman governor with his back ripped open and bleeding, Jesus flatly refused to relinquish the fact that the government of God is for here and now. As he told Pilate: "My kingdom is not of this world. If it were, my servants would fight to prevent my arrest by the Jews. But now my kingdom is from another place" (John 18:36).

In other words, Jesus told Pilate that his kingdom of peace and love does not originate of "this world" of violence, avarice and greed. It originates from God. Thus, Jesus will not resort to the tactics of rulers such as Pilate and maintain power by force. Jesus' government points to another way.

Undermining the Establishment

This was characteristic of how Jesus spoke truth to power amidst the incredible tension and pressure of the times. But Christ's response to the powers-that-be naturally flowed from the cruelty and domination which the Roman Empire inflicted on its subjects, including the Jewish people.

Terror and vengeance were the hallmarks of Rome's so-called *Pax Romana* (or "Roman peace"). The Roman masters were monsters. After viewing the horrific scene of human and animal corpses littering a city destroyed by the Romans, the historian Polybius wrote: "It seems to me that they do this for the sake of terror." Deterrence by terrorism was practiced by Roman warlords and emperors throughout their imperial domination.

Jesus saw the evil in the Roman Empire, and he purposefully drew out such covert evil. In this way, Jesus exposed the dangerous "'spirits,'" Brian McLaren writes in *The Secret Message of Jesus: Uncovering the Truth that Could Change Everything* (2006), "that can inhabit the most respected institutions—*government* (the Roman Empire, Herod's puppet kingdom), *political movements* (Zealots and Herodians), *religious parties* (Pharisees and Sadducees), *religious structures and hierarchies* (chief priests), *professions* (scribes), and *family systems*."

Thus, just as sick, destructive spirits can take possession of people and groups, Jesus offered a new spirit; one that was healthy and creative and promoted a new sense of community. This new kingdom, even today, "represents a counterforce, a countermovement, a counterkingdom, that will," as McLaren argues, "confront all corrupt human regimes, exposing them, naming them, and showing them for what they really are."

But Jesus' kingdom was not like its counterparts. It doesn't force itself where it is not wanted or welcomed. For all its power and reality, it arrives subtly, gently and without great fanfare.

Such a kingdom was seen as a threat to the powers-that-be. In this respect, we should keep in mind that the Romans labeled activists, protesters and actual criminals to more serious insurgents and rebels as "bandits." This meant they were enemies of the Empire.

It is not surprising that when Jesus' teachings promised a kingdom of love and peace that would transcend and eventually undermine the kingdom of violent oppression, he spearheaded a popular movement. The Jewish peasant class had come to despise Roman rule, and many had also come to question the validity of the Temple priests who had the support of the Empire.

A pivotal example of Jesus' subtle undermining of the establishment and its taxation policies came when the Pharisees attempted to entrap Jesus with a question about whether the tribute to Rome was lawful. The Pharisees knew very well that it was not lawful, according to Mosaic law, to pay tribute to Rome.

And they also knew that not to pay tribute would have been seen as rebellion by the Romans and would have been suicidal on Jesus' part. Remember that the Romans claimed divine authority to rule. On the denarius to which Jesus eventually refers is the inscription, "Tiberius Caesar Augustus, Son of the Divine Augustus."

Jesus avoids the trap by responding, "Give to Caesar what is Caesar's, and to God what is God's" (Matthew 22:21). When the Pharisees and other detractors heard this, "they were amazed" (Matthew 22:22). But why were they amazed? The surface interpretation to Jesus' response is simple enough. Pay the tax to the government and the rest to God's work. However, is that what Jesus really said?

First, Jesus' dry response to the question implies that although Caesar may have a right to political rule, that right cannot be based on any claim of divinity. It is blasphemy. Only God possesses the right to divine rule. This answer embodies Jesus' challenge to earthly powers and pretentious actions.

Second, Jesus does not answer when asked, "Is it right to pay taxes to Caesar?" (Matthew 22:17). His answer would have been understood in the way virtually every Israelite listening would have understood, including the Pharisees who were, in effect, on the payroll of the Romans, which was derived from such taxes. That is why they were so amazed or shocked.

What Jesus was saying was that if God is the exclusive Lord and master, then all things belong to God. The implications for Caesar are rather obvious. He is an illegitimate usurper of God's place. "Jesus is clearly and simply reasserting the Israelite principle that Caesar, or any imperial ruler," writes Richard Horsley in *Jesus and Empire: The Kingdom of God and the New World Disorder* (2003), "has no claim on the Israelite people, since God is their actual king and master."

But Jesus did not stop with the Romans. He spoke out against religious corruption, and his main opponents were religious leaders. In fact, he raised urgent warnings against the abuse of religious power.

Above all, Jesus attacked the arrogance of the Jewish religious leaders who were not only in league with the Romans but were supported by them. Jesus attacked this incestuous relationship of the sacred and profane. Jesus would as well, in my opinion, apply the same standard to Christians today who align with governmental power.

Jesus set the standard for confronting the powers-that-be. And many great dissenters have followed his example—from better-known men such as Dietrich Bonhoeffer, Mahatma Gandhi and Martin Luther King to the lesser-known dissenters who resisted the former Soviet Empire to the brave Christians persecuted in China today for simply wanting to worship in their homes independent of the state-controlled church.

Jesus' kingship and rule stand against such things as empires, controlling people, state violence and power politics. Jesus challenged the political and religious belief systems of his day. And worldly powers feared Jesus, not because he challenged them for control of thrones or government but because he undercut their claims of supremacy.

Jesus taught that God was love and that God preferred the poor and downtrodden over the powerful and rich. He said that what is valued in the kingdom of God is not material prosperity but poverty of spirit and mercy. His principles, thus, undermined the establishment and the status quo, not only of his own time but ours as well. And he spoke truth to power in a time when doing so could—and often did—cost a person his life.

As Christians, we all have a duty to speak truth to power. In fact, Christians should be the stewards of freedom. Yet protecting our freedoms will require more than voting. Without a basic knowledge of our rights as citizens—polls indicate that most Americans, for example, know very little about the United States Constitution and Bill of Rights—substantive changes within the government and society will most likely pass unnoticed. As historian Chalmers Johnson writes in his book *Nemesis: The*

Last Days of the American Republic (2006), "The United States today is like a cruise ship on the Niagara River upstream of the most spectacular falls in North America. A few people on board have begun to pick up a slight hiss in the background, to observe a faint haze of mist in the air or on their glasses, to note that the river current seems to be running slightly faster. But no one yet seems to have realized that it is almost too late to head for shore."

There is still enough of the older ethical base in such countries as the United States and Great Britain—what has been called the "Christian memory"—that people will resist if they understand that their values are being seriously threatened. But if this trend toward government control through manipulation continues to move slowly and quietly, there may be less resistance because perceived change is gradual.

Temptation of Christ

There is a temptation to believe that the problems we face today could be resolved if only we had enough money, if only we had enough fame, if only we had enough power. In many ways, the temptations faced by Christians today are no different from those presented to and rejected by Christ. The difference is that which Jesus resolutely turned down in the wilderness—materialism, celebrity and political power—finds many takers among those who call themselves Christians.

As Luke 4 recounts, after his baptism by John, Jesus moved to the wilderness where he fasted and was confronted by Satan, who presented him with three temptations. The first temptation invited Jesus to turn stones into bread, thereby abolishing hunger and otherwise benefiting humankind. The second enticed him to accept the kingdoms of this world. This gift of political power would enable Jesus to establish a kingdom of heaven here on earth, wherein humankind could live happily and properly ever after. The third beguiled him to leap from the top of the Temple without harming himself. For this, he would have achieved celebrity, thus attracting the world's attention to his message.

Jesus rejected all three offers. He recognized that providing unlimited bread to people would make them believe they could live by bread alone. This was a preview of our modern materialistic, affluent society where, in essence, there is no need for God. It is also epitomized by the prosperity gospel, which promotes the idea that the goal of Christians in life is to store treasures for themselves here on earth.

In seeking celebrity, people often come to see themselves as more than people. And the show becomes all-important, as glitzy spectacles and impressive appearances are vital to worldly success. This may be one reason Jesus generally told people to be quiet about the healings and, thus, the signs and wonders. Indeed, you would think that miracles would be the greatest marketing method ever invented. Thus, the reality of the itinerant preacher from Galilee, who avoided such self-marketing, would be quite boring in the television age. But Jesus rejected celebrity for obvious reasons. Indeed, those showcased on television often become gods as they are touted and celebrated. But Jesus knew that we should worship the true God, not one made in our image.

This can be no better illustrated than by the rise of celebrity preachers and televangelists. Although a television preacher may talk about God, God is an off-stage, invisible character, while the television preacher stands center stage and is all too visible. "On these shows," professor Neil Postman writes in *Amusing Ourselves to Death: Public Discourse in the Age of Show Business* (1985), "the preacher is tops. God comes out as second banana."

Moreover, in his book *Christ and the Media* (1979), Malcolm Muggeridge asks:

> Would St. Paul, when he was at Corinth, have agreed to deliver an address during an interval in the games, which were so like television today, being essentially purveyors of

spectator violence and spectator eroticism? Supposing there had been a fourth temptation when our Lord encountered the Devil in the wilderness—this time an offer of networked TV appearance, in prime time, to proclaim and expound his Gospel. Would this offer, too, have been rejected like the others? If so, why?

Obviously, with Jesus' charisma and a few miracles performed on live television, he would have been a sensation. In fact, as Muggeridge has the fictional Gradus, the television promoter who works for Lucifer, Inc., say of Jesus: "It'll put him on the map, launch him on a tremendous career as a worldwide evangelist, spread his teaching throughout the civilized world, and beyond. He'd be crazy to turn it down."

But Jesus did in fact turn such a temptation down. Why? Because Jesus was concerned with truth and reality, not fantasy, images and seeking power.

Finally, accepting political power would have brought Jesus down to the level of the Caesars of his day who proclaimed themselves divine. All in all, what was really at risk in all the temptations was the greatest gift Jesus brought us both when he came into the world and by way of the cross—our true freedom. And Jesus knew that the temptations placed before him all led to the same end—slavery and death.

The Answers Are Spiritual, Not Political or Material

Thus, Jesus recognized that the problems we face will not be solved through money, fame or the political system—and especially not through politics. Although it is a valued and necessary part of the process in a democracy, the ballot box is not the answer to mankind's ills. And Christians who place their hope in a political answer to the world's ills often become nothing more than another tool in the politician's toolbox. Indeed, Jesus refused any type of involvement with political figures.

The fact that Jesus was killed for claiming to be king of the Jews was not an afterthought pinned on the cross above his head. The Roman soldiers commissioned to prepare him for execution knew this was the issue. That is why they gave him the burlesque of coronation, clothing him in royal purple with a mock crown and scepter. Then they abased themselves and called out, "Hail, king of the Jews!" (John 19:3). Afterward, they beat Jesus.

Unfortunately, through the centuries, those claiming to be Jesus' followers, from Christian emperors to popes to those who claimed the divine right of kings, have clothed themselves in his execution robes. Now many evangelical Christians emulate this as well, along with attempts to gain political power. "All have dressed Jesus in borrowed political robes," writes Gary Wills in *What Jesus Meant* (2006). "They will not listen to the gospels, where Jesus clearly says that his reign is not of this present order of things. The political power they claim to exercise in his name is a parody of his claims, like the mock robe and crown put on him by the Roman soldiers. These purported worshipers of Jesus are doing the work of Pontius Pilate."

Former United States House of Representatives Majority Leader Dick Armey, remarking about those who want to impose their version of "righteousness" on others through the hammer of law, wrote in October 2006, "Our movement must avoid the temptations of power and those who would twist the good intentions of Christian voters to support policies that undermine freedom and grow government."

The influential Christian theologian Francis Schaeffer went one step further when he stated that Christians must avoid joining forces with the government. "We must not confuse the Kingdom of God with our country," Schaeffer writes in *A Christian Manifesto* (1981). "To say it another way, 'We should not wrap Christianity in our national flag.'"

Is there a better way than politics to affect the morality of the country? Some believe so. As columnist Cal Thomas, a former vice president of the Moral Majority, remarks, "Conversion is a better avenue to changing one's mind about 'social issues' than power politics because no mind is changed after his or her 'side' is defeated in one election. The person whose party has lost merely fights harder to defeat the people on the winning side in the next election. But change a heart and you potentially can change a mind. Such an approach may not raise funds for an organization, but in large numbers (as we've seen from revivals of the past), it can change the direction of a nation. Isn't that the intended goal of 'Christian activism'?"

We must be ever mindful of the art to which politics and governmental manipulation have developed. Politics is beguiling. And Christians, in particular, must be mindful not to become so closely aligned with politics and the political establishment that they are co-opted by it. Jesus did not confuse the kingdom of God with the kingdom of this world. Accepting political power would have brought Jesus down to the level of the Caesars of his day who proclaimed themselves divine.

And yet, equipped with their own media empires and lobbying entities, evangelical Christian leaders have made no effort to hide their intentions to impact the political scene in the halls of Congress. As Christian Right spokesperson Ann Coulter has remarked, "I'm a Christian first and a mean-spirited, bigoted conservative second, and don't you ever forget it."

Evangelical David Kuo in his book *Tempting Faith: An Inside Story of Political Seduction* (2006) argues that these leaders are nothing more than political tools used by politicians to advance their own agendas. For example, Kuo, who served as Special Assistant to President George W. Bush, noted that evangelical leaders were often invited to White House functions in an effort to curry their favor and garner their support. Conference calls were held in the White House to update Christian leaders. According to Kuo, talking points were distributed and advice was solicited from these Christian leaders and others. But "[t]hat advice rarely went much further than the conference call." And "the true purpose of these calls was to keep prominent social conservatives and their groups or audiences happy."

Thus, appearances were deceptive as key White House staff often ridiculed these same leaders behind their backs. As Kuo recognized, the political establishment just wanted access to the evangelical voting base.

Moreover, although American evangelicals seem to "have amassed greater political power than at any time in our history," as professor Charles Marsh noted in a *New York Times* editorial (January 20,

2006), they seem to be having little impact on the moral structure of the country. In fact, all indications are that since the rise of the Christian Right in the early 1980s, the moral condition of America has worsened. As a Barna Group study concluded, "[M]ost people associated with the Christian faith do not seem to have embraced biblical moral standards. Things are likely to get worse before they get better—and they are not likely to get better unless strong and appealing moral leadership emerges to challenge and redirect people's thoughts and behavior. At the moment, such leadership is absent."

People such as Ann Coulter, a darling of right-wing talk shows, have a tendency to demonize their opponents that is, sadly, typical of many outspoken Christian political leaders today. As Susan Estrich points out in *Soulless: Ann Coulter and the Right-Wing Church of Hate* (2006), Coulter "has called the 9/11 widows 'witches' and 'harpies,' referred to Muslims as 'ragheads,' called Al Gore a 'total fag,' and said that both *New York Times* editor Bill Keller and antiwar congressman Jack Murtha deserved to die."

Whether such hateful bombasts are sincere reflections of how they feel or just ploys to stir up supporters and shore up their funding base is open to question, but I do know that such remarks leave one with the impression that strident partisan politics and a philosophy of hate supersede what Jesus taught about loving one's fellow human beings.

CHAPTER FOUR
Love Your Enemies

In the literal sense, the Bible is the Word of God. If, however, it were recorded in images of words, it would be not the Word, but the image of God. In this sense, when the Children of Israel turned aside from God and made a golden calf, they may be said to have televised him.

—Malcolm Muggeridge,
   Christ and the Media (1977)

Love your enemies, do good to those who hate you, bless those who curse you, pray for those who mistreat you.

—Luke 6:27-28

As history illustrates, there has been a violent, bloody history connected with some past "Christian" regimes. During these times, it was not only wise to fear those who called themselves Christians but to steer clear of them as well. This is recognized by many outside the faith. For example, Oxford University professor Richard Dawkins, one of the world's leading geneticists, is a confirmed atheist who asserts in his book *The God Delusion* (2006) that "there are lots of people out there who have been brought up in some religion or other, are unhappy in it, don't believe it, or are worried about the evils done in its name."

However, while these tragedies happened hundreds of years ago, the vitriol of the so-called Christian Right has forced the fear of Christians to resurface. Jesus exhorted his followers to love their neighbors and turn the other cheek. And yet many Christians—especially those in the media spotlight—are often determined to sow seeds of discord. Rather than setting the standard for loving others, they seem content to hate whole classes of people.

The hatred and animosity exhibited by some Christian leaders toward fellow human beings is the opposite of what Jesus taught. Jesus said: "Love your enemies, do good to those who hate you, bless those who curse you, pray for those who mistreat you. If someone strikes you on one cheek, turn to him the other also." And: "Do not judge, and you will not be judged. Do not condemn, and you will not be condemned. Forgive, and you will be forgiven" (Luke 6:27-29, 37).

Jesus also said: "By their fruit you will recognize them" (Matthew 7:16). Yet, it is clear that the efforts of the Christian Right have had little, if any, impact on American moral values. And if the actions of these leading Christians are anything to go by, the church today seems to be less about love and forgiveness than about vengeance and hatred. As Shane Claiborne writes in his book *The Irresistible Revolution: Living as an Ordinary Radical* (2006), the goal of the Christian should be "to speak the truth in love. There are a lot of people speaking truth with no love."

As we shall see, it is the way in which those who claim to be Christians express themselves and attempt to force their views through intimidation tactics and power politics that causes concern. Indeed, those within the Christian Right are not shy about expressing their views on a litany of topics, sometimes using their religion like a sledgehammer to beat down their opponents. For example, shortly following the 9/11 terrorist attacks, a well-known minister and leader in the Christian Right appeared on *The 700 Club*. The attacks, he said, were evidence that God was angry at America for its cultural immorality, and the nation was paying the price for it. This meant that the 2,645 innocent people killed in the World Trade Center were part of God's penalty. And the blame was laid on certain groups and individuals. "The ACLU's got to take a lot of blame for this." Moreover, "Throwing God out successfully with the help of the federal court system, throwing God out of the public square, out of the schools. The abortionists have got to bear some burden because God will not be mocked. And when we destroy forty million little innocent babies, we make God mad. I really believe that the pagans, and the abortionists, and the feminists, and the gays and the lesbians who are actively trying to make that an alternative lifestyle, the ACLU, People for the American Way—all of them who have tried to secularize America—I point the finger in their face and say 'you helped this happen.'"

This brand of religion—proud of its virtue, self-righteous, quick to judge and condemn, ready to impose burdens rather than share or lift them—is exactly the kind of religion that Jesus opposed. "Any that exalts its own officers, proud of its trappings, building expensive monuments to itself," writes Gary Wills in *What Jesus Meant*. "Any that neglects the poor and cultivates the rich, any that scorns outcasts and flatters rulers."

"I Lived with Fear"

In a 2006 article for *Christianity Today*, I wrote about a decorated American soldier, Patrick Stewart, who had been killed in action in Afghanistan. His wife was engaged in a battle with the Department of Veterans Affairs to have the Wiccan pentacle, a five-pointed star surrounded by a circle, placed on her husband's memorial plaque. Approved religious symbols include those of Christianity, Judaism, Islam and Hinduism, as well as more obscure religions like Konko-Kyo Faith and Seicho-No-le. Symbols are also included for humanism and atheism—but not Wicca.

In the article, I reminded readers that if we are to keep faith with Sgt. Stewart and the other brave men and women who have died in service to the United States, we must remember that all rights hang together. That is both the genius and strength of the American system.

While I expected criticism from conservatives and Christians, I did not foresee the hundreds of emails that came pouring in from Wiccans across the country and around the world. One was particularly moving:

I've lived with the fear of not being Christian all my life. I've been threatened, put down and even suffered violence on more than one occasion and, worse than that, I've seen it happen to those closest to me, as though it were a punishment for believing differently than the majority of those around us. Because of this, I've lived every second of my life until tonight with complete assurance in my own mind that Christians were evil. Not their beliefs, many Pagans respect and even follow Jesus (Yeshua), but Christians themselves. Not for what they believe, but for how they act. I was so ready to believe this whole-heartedly to my dying day. But then something unexpected happened. I read your article. As I read through it, I didn't realize it had come from a Christian. It wasn't until I'd gotten halfway through with it that it really hit me: This is a Christian calling for Pagan equality. By the end of the email, I was in tears, so touched by the kindness you've shown with your words. I can honestly say I'm a changed woman. I'm still afraid of Christians, from experience of course, but I've got hope now that there are some out there who are capable of looking past the separation of our different faiths, and that's something I never thought I'd experience. So I just wanted to thank you for that.

Thus, despite Jesus' teachings on love and compassion, the perceived meanness and hatred of many who call themselves Christians causes fear, apprehension and concern to many non-Christians. In fact, the mean-spirited statements and actions of various Christians have, as I've noted, led some to label them the "American Taliban."

A Duty to Love

Yet among the principles that Jesus taught was the duty to love our fellow human beings. In fact, that four-letter word—love—is the most potent force in human existence because it acts to exalt human beings and works to bring justice into the world.

Indeed, Jesus sought to bring to bear in his own time principles that would affect how people behaved and lived. Jesus not only wanted to rescue people spiritually, he wanted a renewal of community and family life. Unlike the pie-in-the-sky religion practiced by many evangelicals, Jesus had both feet on the ground. In fact, he equates heaven's reign and his personal presence. Jesus says his kingdom is "near" (Matthew 4:17). It is not some distant reality. What has been seen as impossible cannot only be possible, but actual. Jesus' miracles are meant to prove this: "But if I drive out demons by the finger of God, then the kingdom of God has come to you" (Luke 11:20).

The "gospel" or "good news" is that the Messiah has arrived—here and now. This is why Jesus was both ready and willing to help with the pressing needs of his day. God's reign is what Jesus brought to us.

Jesus, as Christians should be today, was a demonstration of the existence of a loving God. However, when there is nothing to be seen but a sea of lovelessness, the concept of a loving God drowns as well.

Although much of what Jesus said consisted of familiar Jewish sayings of the time, it was how he "acted" that was different. It was less what Jesus said than what he did that drew people to him. "Jesus' spiritual ministry was no less in the context of what he preached than in his religious behavior and attitude toward God and the law," writes Harvard professor Orlando Patterson in his book *Freedom* (1991). "There is a markedly essential quality in Jesus' approach to religion. His most striking peculiarity was his approach to ritual purity. He ate what his more orthodox fellow Jews considered unclean food, and enjoyed drinking wine to a degree that was offensive to any rabbi." And he reached out and associated with those considered to be outcasts: "Worse, he associated with riffraff and deviants of all sorts—prostitutes, publicans, and imperial tax collectors. His public informality with children and women was a great scandal to his fellow Jewish contemporaries."

Jesus understood what it meant to be an outcast because he was one himself. When his public life became controversial, as the Gospel of John tells us, "even his own brothers did not believe in him" (John 7:5). After engaging in controversy elsewhere, Jesus tried to return to Nazareth, his native village. But the citizens there "got up, drove him out of town, and took him to the brow of the hill on which the town was built, in order to throw him down the cliff" (Luke 4:29). Clearly, Jesus knew what it felt like to be alone and despised. Vicious rumors were spread about Jesus by those who hated him. He was even accused of being demonic.

Jesus was not part of either the religious or political establishment. He was a loner and a radical. Jesus didn't have an organization or a church for which he raised money. He had no need, therefore, to beg for money or manipulate others in order to get it. He rejected the materialism of the Temple and of the Romans. In fact, as far as we know, he had no money because when he was asked whether it was lawful to pay taxes, Jesus had to ask for a coin (Matthew 22:17-21).

Jesus was not a religious person. Instead, Jesus taught the need for spirituality. As he says, "Spirit gives birth to spirit. You should not be surprised at my saying, 'You must be born again.' The wind blows wherever it pleases. You hear its sound, but you cannot tell where it comes from or where it is going. So it is with everyone born of the Spirit" (John 3:6-8).

Some years later, the Apostle Paul beseeched the Galatian Christians to "live by the Spirit" (Galatians 5:16). He warned them not to go the way of a world still dominated by the Roman Empire. "Those who belong to Christ Jesus," Paul indicates, will exhibit "the fruit of the spirit" which is "love, joy, peace, patience, kindness, goodness, faithfulness, gentleness and self-control" (Galatians 5:22, 24). This is to be the lifestyle of the spirit-filled believer.

Clearly, the "Christianity" that many profess today does not align with the admonition of Paul; nor does it align with the portrait of a humble and compassionate Jesus painted in the Gospels or as depicted by historians. But Jesus recognized that there would be those who *seem* to believe the right things and do religious deeds on behalf of him. These, he said, would be renounced because they didn't love the homeless, the hungry, the poor and the prisoners (Matthew 7:21-23; 41-46). Today, the list of unloved outcasts would probably include those labeled "sinners" and targeted for scorn and damnation by many in the evangelical church.

Atheists for Jesus

Sadly, many evangelicals have forfeited their spiritual mission for a bowl of political porridge. As a consequence, the evangelical church has little impact on the decline of traditional morality in the culture-at-large. And it has even less to do with Jesus' teachings and increasingly resembles something many people want to avoid. If Richard Dawkins had his way, this confirmed atheist might do away entirely with what passes for religion today. "Imagine, with John Lennon, a world with no religion," writes Dawkins in *The God Delusion*. "Imagine no suicide bombers, no 9/11, no 7/7, no Crusades, no witch-hunts, no Gunpowder Plot, no Indian partition, no Israeli/Palestinian wars, no Serb/Croat/Muslim massacres, no persecution of Jews as 'Christ-killers,' no Northern Ireland 'troubles,' no 'honour killings,' no shiny-suited bouffant-haired televangelists fleecing gullible people of their money ('God wants you to give 'till it hurts'). Imagine no Taliban to blow up ancient statues, no public beheadings of blasphemers, no flogging of female skin for the crime of showing an inch of it."

Dawkins, however, is not so much anti-Jesus as he is anti-religion. As he writes in *The God Delusion*, Jesus "was surely one of the great ethical innovators of history. The Sermon on the Mount is way ahead of its time. His 'turn the other cheek' anticipated Gandhi and Martin Luther King by two thousand years. It was not for nothing that I wrote an article called 'Atheists for Jesus' (and was delighted to be presented with a T-shirt bearing the legend)."

Richard Dawkins is not alone in recognizing the lovelessness of the church. If there is to be any true hope for our torn world, it will mean recapturing the heart of Jesus' teachings about loving our enemies. "Along the way of life, someone must have sense enough to cut off the chain of hate," Martin Luther King once wrote. "This can be done by projecting the ethic of love to the center of our lives."

Love Among Believers

I am the first to admit that living a truly Christian life in the present morally chaotic age is a difficult and demanding task. But I also know that there is one element of Christianity without which even the most vibrant faith, the most fearless posture, the most brilliant apologetic and the most selfless service is incomplete. That element is love.

When Jesus was asked which was the greatest commandment in the law, he replied that it was to love God with all your heart, soul and mind and to love your neighbor as yourself (Matthew 22:35-40). Jesus also said in John 13:34-35:

A new command I give you: Love one another. As I have loved you, so you must love one another. By this all men will know that you are my disciples, if you love one another.

As Francis Schaeffer writes in *The Mark of the Christian* (1970):

In the midst of the world, in the midst of our present culture, Jesus is giving a right to the world. Upon His authority He gives the world the right to judge whether you and I are born-again Christians on the basis of our observable love toward all Christians.

In other words, if people challenge whether or not believers are Christians because they have not shown love toward other Christians, it must be understood that they are only exercising a prerogative that Jesus Christ gave them. Schaeffer also adds:

We must not get angry. If people say, "You don't love other Christians," we must go home, get down on our knees, and ask God whether or not what they say is true. And if it is, then they have a right to have said what they said.

In the midst of Christ's prayer in John 17:21, he prays "that all of them may be one, Father, just as you are in me and I am in you. May they also be in us so that the world may believe that you have sent me." Here Christ is praying for oneness among Christians; that is, that Christians love one another.

Note the reason for this unity: "That the world may believe that thou hast sent me." This means that love is the ultimate apologetic, or persuasion to the world. We simply cannot expect the world to believe that the Father sent the Son unless the world sees the reality of Jesus Christ in believers.

CHAPTER FIVE

All That God's Love Means

Perhaps the only thing humans alone can do is be humble. That said, the only way I've ever known to express humility, without turning it instantly into a form of pride, is to give help graciously or graciously to accept it.

—Garret Keizer, *Help: The Original Human Dilemma* (2004)

My command is this: Love each other as I have loved you.

—John 15:12

Love is no easy task. "Now that I come to think of it," writes C. S. Lewis in *Mere Christianity* (1943), "I have not exactly got a feeling of fondness or affection for myself, and I do not even always enjoy my own society. So apparently 'Love your neighbor' does not mean 'feel fond of him' or 'find him attractive.'" Nor apparently does it mean always being nice to other people.

So often I've heard it said that we are to hate what a person does, but we are not to hate the person—that is, hate the sin but not the sinner. But how can I hate what a man does and not hate the man? As Lewis realized, "it occurred to me that there was one man to whom I had been doing this all my life—namely myself. However much I might dislike my own cowardice or conceit or greed, I went on loving myself."

We can love our fellow human beings, no matter how incapable they may seem, by realizing how we forgive our own inadequacies. Thus, in the biblical sense, I can love my neighbor by wishing him well and working for his good but not necessarily feeling fond of him or saying he is nice when he is not or challenging him when he does bad things. This rule applies whether it is Christian facing Christian or Christian facing non-Christian, or vice versa.

This means, as Lewis tells us, "loving people who have nothing lovable about them. But then, has oneself anything lovable about it? You love it simply because it is yourself. God intends us to love all selves in the same way and for the same reason, but He has given us the sum already worked out on our own case to show us how it works. We then go on and apply the rule to all other selves. Perhaps it makes it easier if we remember how He loves us. Not for any nice, attractive qualities we think we have but just because we are the things called selves. For there is really nothing else in us to love."

To reflect their love for God, believers must love others—*all* people—as they love themselves. This love is effectively described and defined in I Corinthians 13:4-8:

> Love is patient, love is kind. It does not envy, it does not boast, it is not proud. It is not rude, it is not self-seeking, it is not easily angered, it keeps no record of wrongs. Love does not delight in evil but rejoices with the truth. It always protects, always trusts, always hopes, always perseveres. Love never fails.

Love in the Christian sense "never fails" because it is a demonstration of who God is. This means that we don't necessarily have to like how people behave or what they do, just as God often doesn't like how we live and what we do. We love others because God created them and, thus, they deserve our respect and help.

Love, therefore, requires an "otherness," a focus away from oneself, a total respect for others as a way of reflecting Christ. This is the kind of expression and action that draws people toward the truth. It concerns what we may call "humanness." Indeed, a primary task for Christians is keeping humanness in the human race—that is, to upgrade and then maintain the individual person's high place in the universe. This is being a God-centered humanist.

All people bear the image of God and have value, not simply because they may or may not happen to be Christians but because they are God's creation and are made in God's image. Modern men and women who have rejected this truth often have no clue as to why they exist or their place in the universe. Because of this, they often feel lost and find life absurd as they, along with many Christians, drown in materialism.

Modern culture further degrades and depersonalizes people. Indeed, if human beings are only the consequence of the impersonal plus time and chance, then why are we really any different than, say, a pig or a goat? Why not treat us merely as "consumers" of what modern corporations offer, no matter how squalid? Why shouldn't televangelists do the same and manipulate their audiences into supporting their extravagant lifestyles? Things such as this, whether done by Christians or others, totally dehumanize people.

The Christian believer, however, should know the value of people as God's creation and act on that knowledge. All people are our neighbors. We are to love all people as ourselves, even if they are not believers and even if the cost of such loving is great.

This means that Christians must show love toward *all* fellow human beings. For example, in order to demonstrate the infinite, personal, loving nature of God, Christians must truly love others as they love themselves.

This same love must be exhibited to all who are considered as outcasts or immoral by Christians. Because all people, Christian or not, are created in the image of God, they must be treated with the same respect as God's other creatures. That means not manipulating or treating them as if they are beneath us. It also means showing compassion. But it does not at the same time mean moving away from Christian truth into modern permissive society. One can deal with anyone with compassion and not completely alienate him if he is met at a genuine human level, as a unique person, and shown the love of Christ.

Sacrificial Giving, Not Materialism

Jesus advocated for the poor and homeless. After all, he was poor. Yet I have witnessed astonishing levels of greed and crass materialism from those who claim to follow Jesus. Truly, what do jet-setting preachers and televangelists of modern Christendom have in common with the itinerant preacher whose followers belonged to the lower classes and the despised trades? To the impartial observer, they would seem to have very little in common with Jesus, whose entire focus was on self-denial and helping the poor.

In fact, Jesus was homeless during his public life and depended on others for shelter. He said it was the meek and the poor who would be blessed—but not with material possessions. Yet the so-called "prosperity gospel," a materialistic philosophy being touted by many popular television preachers and mega-churches, stands in stark contrast to Jesus' attitude toward materialism.

The disciples of Jesus and those of the early church led lives of humility. Unlike the massive church edifices that dot the landscape today, early Christians worshiped in homes and possessed a spiritual power that transformed the world. Contrast this with the revenue of one Texas church, which brings in $77 million annually. When this Houston-based church moved into its new headquarters in a former sports stadium, church officials spent $95 million on renovations, which include two waterfalls and enough carpeting to cover nine football fields. The church, which appears to have more in common with a shopping mall than a place of worship, also boasts a café with wireless Internet access, 32 video game kiosks and a vault in which to store donations.

For such high-profile evangelical figures, revenue raising and prosperity preaching do not end at the church doors. In addition to their roles as Sunday service headliners, promulgators of the wealth gospel have made forays into various entertainment outlets, generating publicity and expanding their audiences.

One popular televangelist and his wife own thirty homes across the country, among them a sprawling Texas ranch and two Newport Beach mansions. This couple travels in a $7.2 million, 19-seat Canadair Turbojet and drives luxury cars. They run their empire with 400 employees from walnut-paneled offices with plush velvet furniture. Another televangelist owns two Rolls-Royces, a private Gulfstream jet, a million-dollar Atlanta home and a Manhattan apartment worth more than twice that amount.

Prosperity theologians present themselves as walking testimony to the creed that faith yields monetary fortune. And if their audiences and budgets are great, these preachers' lifestyles are even grander.

Unabashedly reveling in their opulence, they personify the message they promulgate to their audiences.

In view of Jesus Christ's example, Christians should not entertain themselves in million-dollar cathedrals while poverty and death reign a few blocks away. Jesus shunned material wealth and exemplified a life of abnegation. He taught that any comfort in this world pales in comparison to that of the next and indicates a misdirection of focus and energy. In the Sermon on the Mount, Jesus instructed his disciples not to "store up for yourselves treasures on earth," but rather in heaven (Matthew 6:19). He taught that the devout poor would ascend to the kingdom of God (Luke 6:20). When He encountered a rich young ruler seeking to inherit eternal life, Jesus told him to sell his belongings and share the proceeds with the poor so that he might instead enjoy fortune in heaven. The young man's bondage to wealth kept him from being a true follower of Christ, impeded his relationship with God and thereby kept him from salvation. "It is easier for a camel to go through the eye of a needle," Jesus said, "than for a rich man to enter the kingdom of God" (Matthew 19:24).

Jesus spent far more time among the poor than the rich. Although he did not maintain that acquiring wealth renders one unworthy of salvation, he did say that it is worthless relative to the riches of the afterlife. Jesus contrasted the ephemeral pleasures of the here and now with the promise of eternal salvation: "What good is it for a man to gain the whole world, yet forfeit his soul?" (Mark 8:36).

Of course, the teachings of Jesus run contrary to the so-called prosperity gospel where the chief goal is to gain money and material items. As Jesus proclaims, "Blessed are you who are poor, for yours is the kingdom of God" (Luke 6:20). And, "But woe to you who are rich, for you have already received your comfort" (Luke 6:24).

This is not to say that Jesus condemns those who amass material possessions, nor as demanding that Christians sacrifice everything they have to help others in need, which results in self-imposed destitution. Rather, God wants Christians who have sufficient goods to share with those who do not, and at times to do so sacrificially. As Proverbs 30:8 says, "give me neither poverty nor riches, but give me only my daily bread." A believer's priority must always be his or her relationship with Christ, rather than this-world fulfillment.

In many ways, giving is the essence of love. As C. S. Lewis writes in *Mere Christianity*:

I am afraid the only safe rule is to give more than we can spare. In other words, if our expenditure on comforts, luxuries, amusements, etc., is up to the standard common among those with the same income as our own, we are probably giving away too little. If our charities do not at all pinch or hamper us, I should say they are too small. There ought to be things we should like to do and cannot do because our charitable expenditure excludes them.

In other words, giving that is not *sacrificial* is not true giving. But giving is not limited to money or material items. It includes giving time to others, opening one's home and the general giving of oneself to serve others' needs. It means going the extra mile in order to help another.

Giving also means to pay up personally. I have a Jewish friend, a carpenter, who could live quite well. But Henry doesn't because he gives so much of his time to help others. When Hurricane Katrina wreaked havoc throughout the southeastern United States in 2005, Henry traveled to Mississippi and helped rebuild homes. And during his spare time—when he has it—Henry sits and reads to dying cancer patients at the hospital. Here is a non-Christian who is Christ-like. He pays up personally. A similar spirit, if practiced by Christians, would be a true demonstration that a loving God exists.

Compassion

True compassion must start with assisting those who need help the most. For example, why aren't more believers helping the homeless? Why aren't more believers working with AIDS victims? Why aren't more believers visiting nursing homes? Why aren't more Christians battling for the rights and lives of the unborn, infirm and aged? Why aren't more Christians fighting to protect the human rights and freedoms of not only Christians but our fellow citizens? Christians should know that helping with physical needs is a condition precedent to meeting spiritual needs. Indeed, as the Apostle Paul admonishes: "We who are strong ought to bear with the failings of the weak and not to please ourselves" (Romans 15:1). Jesus reminds us that what we do to the least of these, we do to him.

In one of my travels, I met a Christian man who worked as a barber to meet his living expenses. The major amount of his time, however, was spent working without pay at a half-way house for AIDS victims, most of whom were homosexuals. This man told me that when he first sought out what he saw as a ministry opportunity, he was told that Christians were not welcome because they were negative and lacked compassion. So he asked if he could just wash dishes, which he was allowed to do. Eventually, this man worked his way into the living quarters and has since ministered and prayed with dying homosexuals.

This is what true compassion is all about. It has nothing to do with weeping at tragedy, which might be more indicative of sentimentalism. Compassion is bringing justice and mercy to real-life situations.

However, true compassion often has an emotional accompaniment: *outrage*. Outrage is a legitimate reaction for believers who see inhumanity. Unfortunately, the lack of outrage is a striking characteristic of modern Christians who allow poverty and injustice to abound. The materialism that envelops modern Christianity swallows up humanness, leaving us with little empathy for others' pain.

Identification is at the heart of the incarnated Christ. Indeed, as God became man in and through Jesus, he did not become a powerful political figure, a celebrity or a Pentagon general making quick flying inspections on the front lines. To the contrary, he shared the foxholes, knew the risks and felt the enemy fire. No other god has wounds. It is because God identified so fully with us that we can know and trust Him.

Community-ism

The Roman military power established a form of "peace and security" for the imperial elite. However,

Rome's excessive taxation and the extraction of goods (including crops) from its subject people (such as the Jews) often devastated the peasantry. And because the Galileans and Judeans resisted the Romans, they suffered slaughter, enslavement and destruction of their homes and villages. The burdensome economic demands for the multiple layers of rulers in Palestine—including the Temple priests—compounded this impact. Indeed, the New Testament portrays a people heavily plagued by debt, hunger, physical and social paralysis and despair. The foundations of society, such as the family and village community, were disintegrating under the oppressive Roman regime.

The alternative to this was the "community-ism" of Jesus. He acted to heal the negative impact of the Roman Empire because he understood God to be acting already in people's lives and the village communities.

Jesus lived before the development of technology and the assembly line. Unlike modern people, Jesus did not see life in terms of the machine. In Jesus' view, God was connected to all of life and intimately involved in it. Thus, what he saw around him was less like a machine and more like a family.

This fact is forcibly brought home in two particular instances in the New Testament. The first occurred when Jesus' mother and brothers came to see him while he was teaching a large crowd. Someone said to Jesus, "Your mother and brothers are standing outside, wanting to see you." To which Jesus replied, "My mother and brothers are those who hear God's word and put it into practice" (Luke 8:19-21). This is what the family of God is all about.

The other instance came when Jesus was near death as he hung on the cross. Standing near the cross were his mother and other women who had been close to Jesus. As Jesus looked down and saw his mother and one of his disciples, he said: "Dear woman, here is your son." And to the disciple, Jesus said: "Here is your mother" (John 19:25-27).

Here, in two radically different settings, Jesus maintains community. Thus, in striking contrast to the individualistic and often hippie-like image of Christ, Jesus dealt concretely with the people's problems and social relations—even as he faced death. As professor Richard Horsley writes in *Jesus and Empire*:

> He speaks and performs healings and exorcisms in the context of village assemblies or ad hoc gatherings, often with relatives or friends bringing the person to be healed or summoning the healer. His dialogues in "pronouncement stories," many of which are debates with the Pharisees, address issues of

social and economic relations.

The Gospels portray Jesus' mission as focused on village communities. This is where peasant society was embodied. Jesus was a peasant himself—one born of an oppressed people. He dealt with whole communities, not just individuals, and not just with so-called religious concerns. He dealt with the social and economic conditions as well. Jesus and his disciples were there to help the villagers restructure their lives in light of the parasitical devastation heaped on them by their rulers. In fact, his disciples were, as Horsley writes, "to remain in the villages, based in one household, for a period of time. One detects a certain strategy of mission here. Along with their proclaiming the kingdom and performing healings and exorcisms, the envoys appear to be engaged in community organizing, helping the village to get its act together."

And what was the plan to restructure these communities? It is set forth with clarity in chapters 5 through 8 of the Gospel of Matthew, for example, among others. There Jesus establishes principles by which community can be structured even amidst times of oppression and persecution. Love your enemies, give to your needy neighbors, forgive debts, do not worship materialism, don't judge others and so on. In other words, be merciful. That is why, when sick people were seen as unclean and therefore thought to have devils in them, Jesus accepts and nurtures the afflicted and places them back into the community.

The family, which had been hit hard by the onerous society foisted upon the villagers, had obviously been impacted negatively. How to restore this basic institution? Don't even think about adultery. Don't divorce. Love little children. Treat women like human beings, not property. Jesus said he had come to fulfill the law. Thus, as the Ten Commandments require, honor your father and mother.

Love, then, is not a feeling or an attitude. It is putting concrete practices into action in restoring community life—such as canceling debts, mutual sharing and loving all people.

The early gatherings of the early church exemplified community-ism. As Acts 4:32-37 tells us:

> All the believers were one in heart and mind. No one claimed that any of his possessions was his own, but they shared everything they had. With great power the apostles continued to testify to the resurrection of the Lord Jesus, and much grace was upon them all. There were no needy persons among them. For from time to time those who owned lands or houses sold them, brought the money from

the sales and put it at the apostles' feet, and it was distributed to anyone as he had need. Joseph, a Levite from Cyprus, whom the apostles called Barnabas (which means Son of Encouragement), sold a field he owned and brought the money and put it at the apostles' feet.

Help

The essence of love is expressed in helping others. In fact, what defines us as true human beings is the degree to which we help those in need. To follow Christ is to be selfless. And we need a radical unselfishness among Christians that focuses on a non-self-centered otherness if a semblance of true Christianity is to survive in our troubled and torn world. This is the same spirit of unselfishness that moved the Samaritan in the tenth chapter of Luke to act.

Although most of us know the story of the Good Samaritan, it is worth repeating.

One day, a man came to Jesus. This man, a lawyer, wanted to raise some questions about vital matters in life. Among other things, he asked Jesus, "Who is my neighbor?" From the way the lawyer phrased his questions, it was clear that he was trying to trick Jesus. He wanted to show Jesus that he knew a little more than Christ knew and, through this, throw Jesus off-base. The questions could have easily ended up in a philosophical and theological debate.

The Reverend Martin Luther King often found himself in a similar thicket of questions and controversy. On April 3, 1968, the day before he was assassinated, King was in Memphis to help striking sanitation workers get a fair wage. The night before, he spoke to a church audience in Memphis about Christ's dilemma and the questions as posed by the lawyer:

> Jesus immediately pulled that question from mid-air, and placed it on a dangerous curve between Jerusalem and Jericho. And he talked about a certain man, who fell among thieves. You remember that a Levite and a priest passed by on the other side. They didn't stop to help him. And finally a man of another race came by. He got down from his beast, decided not to be compassionate by proxy. But with him, administered first aid, and helped the man in need. Jesus ended up saying, this was the good man, this was the great man, because he had the capacity to project the "I" into the "thou," and to be concerned about his brother.

In our hectic, chaotic lives, it is easy to imagine how the average person, even one wishing to live a life devoted to Christ, can become distracted. And sometimes the often endless stream of church meetings, as Dr. King notes, could very well deter us from helping someone who has fallen by the wayside:

> Now you know, we use our imagination a great deal to try to determine why the priest and the Levite didn't stop. At times we say they were busy going to church meetings—an ecclesiastical gathering—and they had to get on down to Jerusalem so they wouldn't be late for their meeting.

Or maybe the religious rules, which some refer to as legalism, by which we live our lives become a deterrent to being a Good Samaritan. But as Dr. King pointed out, there are other reasons that force some not to help:

> But I'm going to tell you what my imagination tells me. It's possible that these men were afraid. You see, the Jericho road is a dangerous road. I remember when Mrs. King and I were first in Jerusalem. We rented a car and drove from Jerusalem down to Jericho. And as soon as we got on that road, I said to

my wife, "I can see why Jesus used this as a setting for his parable." It's a winding, meandering road. It's really conducive for ambushing. You start out in Jerusalem, which is about 1200 miles, or rather 1200 feet above sea level. And by the time you get down to Jericho, fifteen or twenty minutes later, you're about 2200 feet below sea level. That's a dangerous road. In the days of Jesus it came to be known as the "Bloody Pass."

Fear is often our greatest enemy. It is possible that the priest and the Levite looked over at the man on the ground and wondered if the robbers were still lurking nearby. It is also possible that they believed the man on the ground was faking. In other words, he was merely acting as if he had been robbed and injured in order to lure them close enough to rob them.

One thing is certain. The moment of truth had come. What would they do? Obviously, the first question the Levite asked was, "If I stop to help this man, what will happen to me?"

But the Good Samaritan came by and reversed the question: "If I do not stop to help this man, what will happen to *him*?" That was the question Martin Luther King posed to the Christian audience that night:

That's the question before you tonight. Not, "If I stop to help the sanitation workers, what will happen to all of the hours that I usually spend in my office every day and every week as a pastor?" The question is not, "If I stop to help this man in need, what will happen to me?" "If I do not stop to help the sanitation workers, what will happen to them?" That's the question.

God would, thus, have us be Good Samaritans and help those who are despised and helpless. Indeed, we are in the world to help one another. But what does it mean to help such people? It certainly means more than prayer or paying lip-service to a need.

As Christ tells us, when the Good Samaritan saw the injured man, "he took pity on him" (Luke 10:33). He had *compassion* for this injured soul. This means showing concern for another beyond any negative impact it may have on us or our possessions.

This will necessarily mean helping beyond the minimal. In fact, as Christ recognizes in the parable, the Good Samaritan helped this poor man by bandaging his wounds and taking him to a place where he could be cared for. The Good Samaritan even left money for the injured man's care. In other words, he went far out of his way to help a fellow human being who had fallen on bad times. And as Christ tells his disciples, "Go and do likewise" (Luke 10:37).

Christ provides the model for what we should be as compassionate, caring people. In Matthew 22:37-40, when Jesus was asked which commandment was the most important, he replied:

> "Love the Lord your God with all your heart and with all your soul and with all your mind." This is the first and greatest commandment. And the second is like it: "Love your neighbor as yourself." All the Law and the Prophets hang on these two commandments.

Christ emphasized dedicating one's *whole self* to serving God by loving all people (our neighbors) and treating them with the same measure of love and respect that we believe we deserve. If we strive to accomplish this, we can be of great service to God in accomplishing what any good person should—helping the less fortunate.

Indeed, Christ characterized his own mission in this fashion. In Luke 4:18-19, Christ states:

> The Spirit of the Lord is on me, because he has anointed me to preach good news to the poor. He has sent me to proclaim freedom for

the prisoners and recovery of sight for the blind, to release the oppressed, to proclaim the year of the Lord's favor.

The bottom line is that none of us can exist very long without help from other human beings. This is brought home forcefully in a story that Garret Keizer recounts in his insightful book *Help: The Original Human Dilemma* (2004). Supposedly, in hell, the damned sit around a great pot, all hungry, because the spoons they hold are too long to bring the food to their mouths. In heaven, people are sitting around the same pot with the same long spoons, but everyone is full. Why? Because in heaven, people use their long spoons to feed one another.

CHAPTER SIX
Blessed Are the Peacemakers

I refuse to accept the cynical notion that nation after nation must spiral down a militaristic stairway into the hell of thermonuclear destruction. I believe that unarmed truth and unconditional love will have the final word in reality. This is why right temporarily defeated is stronger than evil triumphant. I believe that even amid today's motor bursts and whining bullets, there is still hope for a brighter tomorrow. I believe that wounded justice, lying prostrate on the blood-flowing streets of our nations, can be lifted from this dust of shame to reign supreme among the children of men.

> —Martin Luther King,
> Nobel Prize Acceptance Speech
> (December 10, 1964)

Make every effort to live in peace with all men and to be holy; without holiness no one will see the Lord.

> —Hebrews 12:14

When Jesus said "Blessed are the peacemakers," exhorting his followers to turn the other cheek and give freely, he was telling us that active peacemaking is the way to end violence. Can you imagine what the world would be like if every church adopted that attitude and focused its energies on active peacemaking?

In dealing compassionately with our fellow human beings, much of what is taught about violence—even by Christians—must be rethought. Jesus opposed violence in all its forms. More than any other teacher of nonviolence, such as Mahatma Gandhi or Martin Luther King, Jesus was adamant in what he forbade. Take, for example, Luke 6:27-38:

> But I tell you who hear me: Love your enemies, do good to those who hate you, bless those who curse you, pray for those who mistreat you. If someone strikes you on one cheek, turn to him the other also. If someone takes your cloak, do not stop him from taking your tunic. Give to everyone who asks you, and if anyone takes what belongs to you, do not demand it back. Do to others as you would have them do to you. If you love those who love you, what credit is that to you? Even "sinners" love those who love them. And if you do good to those who are good to you, what credit is that to you? Even "sin-

ners" do that. And if you lend to those from whom you expect repayment, what credit is that to you? Even "sinners" lend to "sinners," expecting to be repaid in full. But love your enemies, do good to them, and lend to them without expecting to get anything back. Then your reward will be great, and you will be sons of the Most High, because he is kind to the ungrateful and wicked. Be merciful, just as your Father is merciful.

And in Matthew 5:43-48 we read:

You have heard that it was said, "Love your neighbor and hate your enemy." But I tell you: Love your enemies and pray for those who persecute you, that you may be sons of your Father in heaven. He causes his sun to rise on the evil and the good, and sends rain on the righteous and the unrighteous. If you love those who love you, what reward will you get? Are not even the tax collectors doing that? And if you greet only your brothers, what are you doing more than others? Do not even pagans do that? Be perfect, therefore, as your heavenly Father is perfect.

Note specifically that Jesus explicitly extends the Old Testament command to "love your neighbor" to "love your enemies." This is at the heart of the Christian ethic on nonviolence.

This is the essence of spiritual warfare. Truth, not violence, is the great divider. As Jesus says in Matthew 10:34-39:

> Do not suppose that I have come to bring peace to the earth. I did not come to bring peace, but a sword. For I have come to turn a man against his father, a daughter against her mother, a daughter-in-law against her mother-in-law—a man's enemies will be the members of his own household. Anyone who loves his father or mother more than me is not worthy of me; anyone who loves his son or daughter more than me is not worthy of me; and anyone who does not take his cross and follow me is not worthy of me. Whoever finds his life will lose it, and whoever loses his life for my sake will find it.

Tremendous ingenuity has been expended by Christians and non-Christians alike to compromise these uncompromising words. "Jesus is too much for us," Gary Wills writes in *What Jesus Meant*. "The churches' later treatment of the gospels is one long effort to rescue Jesus from 'extremism.' Jesus consistently opposed violence." In fact, Jesus rebuked Peter and ordered him not to use the sword, even to protect his Lord (Matthew 26:52). Jesus then demonstrated the uniqueness of the kingdom he came to give us by healing the soldier's ear—showing that his kingdom would not advance by destroying the enemy who seeks to destroy you. Instead, we are to love and serve, all the while working to transform the enemy who seeks to destroy us.

Nothing better illustrates this principle than Matthew 5:39: "Do not resist an evil person. If someone strikes you on the right cheek, turn to him the other also." From this, you are probably imagining a blow with the right fist. But such a blow would fall on the *left* cheek. To hit the right side with a fist would require the left hand. But the left hand, however, was used for unclean tasks. Indeed, at Qumran, a Jewish religious community of Jesus' day, to gesture with the left hand meant exclusion from the meeting and penance for ten days. Think about it for a moment: how would you hit another person's right cheek with your right hand? If you've tried it, you realize that the only feasible blow is a backhand. But the backhand is not a blow to injure. It was meant to insult, humiliate and degrade. And it was not administered by an equal, but to an inferior. In fact, masters backhanded slaves; husbands, wives; parents, children; Romans, Jews. The whole point of hitting someone in this fashion was to force the person back into place.

The people Jesus addresses are used to being degraded. But he tells them to refuse to accept this kind of treatment and, if backhanded, to turn the other cheek. However, this is the point. "By turning the other cheek," as biblical scholar Walter Wink notes in *The Powers That Be: Theology for a New Millennium* (1998), "the servant makes it impossible for the master to use the backhand again: his nose is in the way. And anyway, it's like telling a joke twice; if it didn't work the first time, it simply won't work. The left cheek now offers a perfect target for a blow with the right fist; but only equals fought with fists, as we know from Jewish sources, and the last thing the master wishes to do is to establish this underling's equality. This act of defiance renders the master incapable of asserting his dominance in this relationship. He can have the slave beaten, but he can no longer cow him."

The moral to the story is that by turning the other cheek, the "inferior" is saying, "I'm a human being, just like you. I refuse to be humiliated any longer. I am your equal. I am a child of God. I won't take this kind of treatment anymore."

As Pastor Gregory Boyd writes in *The Myth of a Christian Nation: How the Quest for Political Power is Destroying the Church* (2005):

To the contrary, Jesus is giving us a way by which we can keep from being defined by those who act unjustly toward us. When we respond to violence with violence, whether it be physical, verbal, or attitudinal, we legitimize the violence of our enemy and sink to his level. When we instead respond unexpectedly—offering our other cheek and going a second mile—we reveal, even as we expose the injustice of his actions, that our nemesis doesn't have the power to define us by those actions. In this sense we serve our enemy, for manifesting God's love and exposing evil (the two always go hand in hand) open up the possibility that he will repent and be transformed.

There are those who claim that violence is sometimes justified and point to the story of Jesus cleansing the Temple by driving out the money changers with a whip of cords (John 2:13-16). But according to Walter Wink, "There Jesus uses it to drive out the sheep and oxen—an act which saves the lives of these sacrificial victims!"

In his crucifixion, Jesus refuses to turn to violence as a last resort but instead trusts God for the outcome. In fact, Christ's crucifixion was a radical repudiation of the use of violent force. And the cross, which was the Roman tool of execution, was reserved especially for leaders of rebellions. "Anyone proclaiming a rival kingdom to the kingdom of Caesar would be a prime candidate for crucifixion," writes Brian McLaren in *The Secret Message of Jesus*. "This is exactly what Jesus proclaimed, and this is exactly what he offered." But Jesus' kingdom was one of peace.

The so-called Roman peace (*Pax Romana*) was made possible by the cross. That is, people so feared crucifixion that many opted not to challenge the emperor rather than face the possibility of death on the cross. Why then would early Christians choose the cross—an instrument of torture, domination, fear, intimidation and death—as their primary symbol? What could this possibly mean?

For early Christians, "it apparently meant that the kingdom of God would triumph not by inflicting violence but by enduring it," notes McLaren, "not by making others suffer but by willingly enduring suffering for the sake of justice—not by coercing or humiliating others but by enduring their humiliation with gentle dignity." Jesus, they believed, had taken the empire's instrument of torture and transformed it into God's symbol of the repudiation of violence. The message? Love, not violence, is the most powerful force in the universe.

Not surprisingly, the early Christians were not

crusaders or warriors, but martyrs—men and women with the faith and courage to face the lions. Like Jesus, they chose to suffer rather than inflict violence.

"Jesus clearly rejected the military option as a way to redress Jewish grievances," writes Wink. "He refused to lead troops in war against Rome, or defend his own cause by violent means." In fact, he endured the cross rather than seek redress in violence. Jesus, thus, discovered a way of opposing evil without becoming evil in the process.

In fact, leaders in the early church adopted Jesus' attitude of nonviolence. Tertullian (born about A.D. 160), one of the giants of the early church, stated very clearly that confessing "Jesus as Lord" means taking the teachings of Jesus seriously. Tertullian asked:

> Shall it be held lawful to make an occupation of the sword, when the Lord proclaims he who uses the sword shall perish by the sword? And shall the son of peace take part in the battle when it does not become him even to sue at law? And shall he apply the chain, and the prison, and the torture, and the punishment, who is not the avenger even of his own wrongs?

In fact, Tertullian had pithy advice for soldiers who converted to Christianity: quit the army or be martyred for refusing to fight. Tertullian was not alone in his thinking. "For three centuries," Walter Wink states, "no Christian author to our knowledge approved of Christian participation in battle." This, of course, changed in the third century when the church was institutionalized and became an integral part of the warring Roman Empire.

The answer, of course, is peace. But peace is not simply a glow word—a longing for a state of peace. Instead, Jesus' principle is dynamic, not a state of being. His insistence is on active *peacemaking*. Jesus said: "Blessed are the peacemakers, for they will be called sons of God" (Matthew 5:9). But peacemaking is not magic. It is a costly positive. We are to love our enemies, but peacemaking invites persecution. "The Son of God requires us to go through barriers that have hitherto led to war, and to be *for* the enemy, for the good, to be in the clinch of love and hug the Russian bear," writes Alan Storkey in *Jesus and Politics*. "This approach is costly, as the Gospels show." Indeed, peacemakers opposing violence will run headlong into a culture that is not only violent but promotes it through the media, through entertainment distractions and through governmental politicians, as well as the military structure.

This is not to say that Jesus was a pacifist. The opposite is true. He spoke truth to power and engaged in active resistance to injustice. In my opinion, Jesus would have intervened to defend someone being violently mistreated, and I believe we must do the same. But he would never have engaged in violence as the means to an end.

Peacemakers, as such, will be forced to speak truth to power. And much like Jesus, the Apostle Paul and the early church, they will, as Martin Luther King once said, be accused of being "disturbers of the peace" and "agitators."

Suffering and Persecution

Why were the Christians thrown to the lions?

Because they were seen as rebels, as those who would defy the state. Even Paul's reference to Jesus being Lord resonates with rebellion. The pledge of citizen allegiance in the Roman Empire was to Caesar as Lord. To say Jesus is Lord is to declare one's allegiance to a different empire or kingdom. This is one reason the early Christians were persecuted—not for their religious beliefs but for their lack of patriotism and national loyalty in refusing to call Caesar Lord.

But Christians are not rebels in the traditional sense. After all, most Christians don't rock the boat and cause political disturbances. They aren't terrorists. To most, they would be considered good, law-abiding citizens. But they are still persecuted in countries worldwide. They're tortured and locked up for wanting to worship God as they see fit—sometimes for merely preaching the Gospel or singing hymns in their homes.

By their very presence, Christians in such countries proclaim that "God rules and you do not." This is a threat to states that rule by bullying their citizens. They rule by coercion, persecution and killing. Christians are seen as political threats in such places. This is because true Christianity requires living before God and "not within the conception of the state or ruler," writes Alan Storkey. "Living before God demythologizes the whole ethos of dominating politics. People are free to live before God as they choose. Politics is pushed into a limited place, and there is room for friendship, science, children, discussion, prayer, the arts, fishing, and walking about, meeting people. The Pharisees want to dominate people's lives with their religio-political rules, but Jesus shrugs them off."

Simply put, the early Christians knew what it was to follow Jesus' example. Jesus was no wimp. He said "No" to the Romans and the Chief Priests without fear and exposed them for the parasitic powers they were. He offered them instead the gentle rule of a servant God, which is beautifully illustrated just before the Last Supper. When Jesus knew that God had given all things to him, he exercised his divine authority as an ultimate act of servanthood to his own disciples. Thus, "he got up from the meal, took off his outer clothing, and wrapped a towel around his waist. After that, he poured water into a basin and began to wash his disciples' feet, drying them with the towel that was wrapped around him" (John 13:4-5).

This is how power is to be wielded in the government of God. The true Christian message then cuts through the power mongering and evil of all political powers. But the response from authoritarian regimes is often brutal.

Thus, Christians who proceed in a manner consistent with true Christianity may not demand or expect to move from victory to victory. Instead, they will suffer persecution. John the Baptist spoke out against corruption in the court of Herod, and his actions cost him his head. Christians can expect the same, or even more violent treatment since modern technology provides persecutors with a variety of new and terrifying alternatives. And believers in foreign lands will find persecution heightened by nationalistic prejudice or the hostility of other religions.

Western Christians currently have it easy. They do not compare well with the first Christians or with those solitary souls throughout the world who are persecuted simply because they are believers who will not be silenced. Unfortunately, American

Christians, trapped within the tentacles of materialism, have told me they would not fight for the freedom to speak the truth because they might lose their jobs.

Then there is the excuse that if one stands for truth, it will offend someone and the Christian will lose his or her chance to preach the gospel. This is a fundamental way of avoiding the difficult task of taking a stand. One may be disliked or ridiculed for speaking the truth, but, in such instances, that person will only be following Jesus' example.

Truth, as such, is precisely what true Christianity has to offer. Curiously, it is often the non-Christian who sees the need for such a standard of truth. For example, the French existentialist Albert Camus, who won the Nobel Prize for literature, claimed to believe in nothing and to consider everything absurd. But Camus was an honest thinker. And perhaps because of this honesty, along with his absence of belief, he was able to see the needs of the age in a way matched by few of his peers. When Camus was asked to speak before a Dominican monastery in 1948, this, in part, is what he had to say:

What the world expects of Christians is that Christians should speak out, loud and clear, and that they should voice their condemnation in such a way that never a doubt, never the slightest doubt, could rise in the heart of the simplest man. That they should get away from abstraction and confront the blood-stained face history has taken on today. The grouping we need is a grouping of men resolved to speak out clearly, and to pay up personally.

Camus clearly believed that the role of the Christian was to speak truth to power and confront the staggering evils perpetrated by the governmental and societal regimes of his day:

We are faced with evil. And, as for me, I feel rather as Augustine did before becoming a Christian when he said: "I tried to find the source of evil and I got nowhere." But it is also true that I, and a few others, know what must be done, if not to reduce evil, at least not to add to it. Perhaps we cannot prevent this world from being a world in which children are tortured. But we can reduce the number of tortured children. And if you don't help us, who else in the world can help us do this?

Thus, Camus urged Christians not only to raise their voices but to do so loudly and in such a way that there is no doubt as to what is being said—that is, "to pay up personally," to practice what Jesus taught. That done, they must stand by what they have said.

Christians should be the vanguard of God's love and truth to the world. It is a faith for anyone who hungers for wisdom, truth and compassion; it is for the person who longs for an antidote to the rampant materialism, corruption and hopelessness that are so much a part of our torn world.

In the final analysis, persecution will follow any strong stand. One must be prepared. And above all, one must count the cost.

Suffering, then, is not an optional choice in the faith but rather an essential aspect of true Christianity. Jesus Christ foretold that the true believer would be hated (John 15:18-19). And he specifically noted that suffering and persecution would follow: "In this world you will have trouble. But take heart! I have overcome the world" (John 16:33).

For Christians, suffering for what is right is never meaningless. Jesus uses suffering as a way to mature and perfect the believer. Hebrews 2:10 reads: "In bringing many sons to glory, it was fitting that God, for whom and through whom everything exists, should make the author of their salvation perfect through suffering." How then shall followers of Jesus Christ escape the need for a similar process?

Suffering is also preparation for the Christian's eventual union with God. "We must go through many hardships," writes the Apostle Paul, "to enter the kingdom of God" (Acts 14:22). Moreover, those who suffer for the sake of righteousness are called blessed (I Peter 3:14) and may rejoice and be glad (Matthew 5:12) because of the prospect of eventual exultation with God.

Practicing true Christianity and living consistently as a Christian is a difficult task that at times seems impossible. The Christian is told to run the race of life "in such a way as to get the prize," but failure is a definite possibility (I Corinthians 9:24). In fact, *we all fail*. That is the human dilemma; that is a reality we cannot escape.

No one is capable of doing everything. However, Christ does not expect the believer to do everything and has assured believers that his yoke is easy and his burden light. Jesus promises to give the Christian rest (Matthew 11:28-29). In short, there is no cause for despair or pessimism.

Who would have thought that a ragtag band of Jewish radicals from an obscure Roman colony could change the course of history? And yet that is precisely what happened. The fact that they prevailed against all odds is an inspiration.

There is, thus, hope.

CHAPTER SEVEN

A Life of Love

He was not ashamed of his disciples, he became
the brother of mankind, and bore their shame
unto the death of the cross. That is how Jesus,
the crucified, was merciful.

   —Dietrich Bonhoeffer,
      The Cost of Discipleship (1937)

If you love those who love you, what reward
will you get?

   —Matthew 5:46

After struggling long and hard with all that Christianity should be and is not, I have come to the following conclusion: God is not dead and He does not hate us, as many claim. And the life and teachings of the humble carpenter from Galilee still have relevance today. They can transform lives from the inside out by winning people to God's sovereign love.

However, we can talk until we're blue in the face about love, but it will all be meaningless unless we practice what we preach. This is the essence of the communication that we should impart to our fellow human beings, as required by Jesus. It is a message of transformation, not rejection. Rejection hardens people and drives them from the truth. But acceptance makes transformation possible. And it is such an acceptance that moves us to love one another, even those who are difficult to love.

Christians, as I've said, are the demonstration of the existence of a loving, personal God—one who cares about His creatures. "But if we as individual Christians, and as a church, act less than a personal relationship to other men," writes Francis Schaeffer in *True Spirituality* (1971), "where is the demonstration that God the Creator is personal?"

In other words, Christians are to be God's reality in this world. We are to demonstrate that when we speak of love, it is not merely words. We are to mean it. Otherwise, those outside the faith will not, and should not, believe that the God we believe in exists.

Indeed, if I act carelessly in how I treat my fellow human beings, I make God out to be a liar. I'm no better than those who are consistent in their malicious treatment of people. Or, as Francis Schaeffer puts it, "If I really love a man as I love myself, I will long to see him to be what he could be on the basis of Christ's work, for that is what I want or what I should want for myself on the basis of Christ's work. And if it is otherwise, not only is my communication with the man broken, but my communication with God as well. For this is sin, breaking Christ's second commandment to love my neighbor as myself."

God's love is, thus, an all-or-nothing love. Along these lines, Paul teaches, "Do everything in love" (I Corinthians 16:14). This means that we should never engage in anything that is not motivated by Christlike love.

We are to "live a life of love, just as Christ loved us and gave himself up for us" (Ephesians 5:2). And above all other virtues, Paul tells us to "put on love" (Colossians 3:14). Peter likewise instructs: "Above all, love each other deeply, because love covers over a multitude of sins" (I Peter 4:8).

When we are on our death beds, we will not be concerned about the condition of our homes or cars. Our bank account will not be on our minds. Nor will our jobs.

In the end, all we have left are human relationships—not only with our family and friends but with those whose lives we touch in infinitely smaller ways. How did we treat the people around us? How much did we reach out and attempt to help those who asked for help? How did we speak of our fellow human beings?

If Christians were to live the life of love that God so desires, the world as we know it could be changed. That is the power of that four-letter word.

John W. Whitehead is an attorney and author who has written, debated and practiced widely in the area of constitutional law and human rights. Whitehead's concern for the persecuted and oppressed led him, in 1982, to establish The Rutherford Institute, a non-profit civil liberties and human rights organization whose international headquarters are located in Charlottesville, Virginia. Whitehead serves as the Institute's president and spokesperson, in addition to writing a weekly commentary that is distributed to several hundred newspapers, Whitehead's aggressive, pioneering approach to civil liberties issues has earned him numerous accolades, including the Hungarian Medal of Freedom.

Born in 1946 in Tennessee, John W. Whitehead earned a Bachelor of Arts degree from the University of Arkansas in 1969 and a Juris Doctorate degree from the University of Arkansas School of Law in 1974. He served as an officer in the United States Army from 1969 to 1971. Whitehead and his wife have five children.

TRI PRESS® is an imprint
of The Rutherford Institute.

The Rutherford Institute is a nonprofit legal and educational organization dedicated to the defense of civil liberties, specializing in religious freedom issues. Deeply committed to protecting the constitutional freedoms of every American and the human rights of all people, the Institute works to ensure that when people's rights are violated, they are treated fairly in the courts and are free to express their beliefs without fear of further recrimination or persecution. To further this goal, the Institute defends those in need without charging them for such services.

For more information about
The Rutherford Institute,
visit
www.rutherford.org

Or write to:
The Rutherford Institute
Post Office Box 7482
Charlottesville, VA 22906-7482